Borderline Personality Disorder

A Guide to Understanding and Managing BPD

© **Copyright 2022 Rivercat Books LLC - All rights reserved.**

The content contained within this book may not be reproduced, duplicated or transmitted without direct written permission from the author or the publisher.

Under no circumstances will any blame or legal responsibility be held against the publisher, or author, for any damages, reparation, or monetary loss due to the information contained within this book, either directly or indirectly.

Legal Notice:

This book is copyright protected. It is only for personal use. You cannot amend, distribute, sell, use, quote or paraphrase any part, or the content within this book, without the consent of the author or publisher.

Disclaimer Notice:

Please note the information contained within this document is for educational and entertainment purposes only. All effort has been executed to present accurate, up to date, reliable, complete information. No warranties of any kind are declared or implied. Readers acknowledge that the author is not engaged in the rendering of legal, financial, medical or professional advice. The content within this book has been derived from various sources. Please consult a licensed professional before attempting any techniques outlined in this book.

By reading this document, the reader agrees that under no circumstances is the author responsible for any losses, direct or indirect, that are incurred as a result of the use of the information contained within this document, including, but not limited to, errors, omissions, or inaccuracies.

Table of Contents

Introduction 1

Chapter 1: FAQs 3

Chapter 2: Symptoms and Diagnosis 6

Chapter 3: Recognizing and Understanding the Triggers 15

Chapter 4: Treatment for Borderline Personality Disorder 23

Chapter 5: Techniques for Helping a Loved One 41

Chapter 6: Setting Healthy Boundaries and Communication . 49

Chapter 7: Self-Help Exercises 65

Conclusion 74

References 75

Introduction

What Is Borderline Personality Disorder?

Borderline Personality Disorder is one of the most misunderstood disorders, and it can be especially difficult for loved ones to cope with and understand. People with Borderline Personality Disorder (BPD) are almost constantly experiencing a whirlwind of emotions. Even the smallest of things can trigger some really strong emotions, which can be incredibly difficult for these people to regulate. Those with BPD also struggle with their self-esteem, goals, and what makes them happy or upsets them. This results in them feeling regularly confused and unsure of their ultimate purpose, which can be emotionally unnerving. Those with BPD also have an intense fear of abandonment, meaning they really struggle to be alone and constantly need reassurance from others.

People with BPD tendencies are typically emotionally volatile and often drive others away, as they do not have the same ability to self-soothe as most others. Instead, they will lose emotional control quickly and find it very difficult to calm down and regain composure. They may also say hurtful things to those around them and behave in unacceptable and impulsive ways when they lose emotional control. This kind of behavior often drives people away, making it very difficult for them to maintain lasting relationships. Even worse, the feelings of intense guilt and shame after the episode only perpetuate this toxic cycle.

As difficult as this condition can be for both the sufferer and their loved ones, this condition can be managed with the correct treatment, time, and patience. If you, or someone close to you, suffers from BPD, then it's important that you take the time to understand the symptoms, diagnoses, and treatment methods so that you can be as understanding and supportive as possible. Later in this book, you will learn about the most common symptoms to look out for if you suspect a loved one has BPD. You will also learn how to handle the situation in the most empathetic and effective manner, so you don't cause further upset.

Chapter 1: FAQs

Since BPD is one of the most misunderstood disorders, I thought I'd start by answering a few of the most frequently asked questions! Those listed below cover some of the most important questions that are not only helpful for the person with BPD, but their loved ones too. By familiarizing yourself with the basics, it will be much easier to take in some of the more complex facts. With this in mind, let's get started!

Five FAQs

How Common is BPD?

BPD is actually not as common as many people think! Interestingly, only 1.4% of people in the United States have BPD, with 75% of them being female. This is not to say that women are necessarily more susceptible to BPD than men, but it appears that men seem to be wrongly diagnosed with depression or PTSD. That said, there may be more people with BPD than have been recorded; they simply haven't been diagnosed.

Many people are afraid to see a psychiatrist for a thorough evaluation as they are too nervous of the judgment that may arise from the outcome, or they may be in denial. Whatever the reason, there are many people still waiting for a diagnosis. Hopefully, this will change in the future as healthcare improves and people are better educated about BPD.

How Can I Best Encourage a Loved One to Get Help?

The key here is not to offend the person in any way. You don't want to make them sound as if they are crazy or out of line, or they definitely will *not* react well! You need to approach the situation in an empathetic and caring manner so that they let down their defenses. Make sure that you listen more than you speak, and try not to make assumptions until you've heard them out. Only speak to them when they are in a calm state, otherwise, you'll make the situation much worse.

Lastly, and most importantly, tell them that you don't like seeing them in pain and you want them to get the help they need to be happy again. If they haven't yet received a diagnosis, explain to them how freeing it will be to understand yourself better and get the help you deserve.

What's the Best Way to Explain BPD?

One of the biggest misconceptions of BPD is that it means the person has multiple personalities. This simply isn't true! The best way to explain BPD is that the person battles to regulate their emotions in the same way most people do. This means that they feel everything deeply and sometimes act in an impulsive manner as a result of these intense feelings. They have an "all-or-nothing" approach to relationships and life in general, which makes them very emotional and sensitive.

How Do I Help a Loved One on a High When They're Not Okay?

One thing to remember about BPD is that the person usually goes from feeling absolutely amazing to feeling really down and out. This inability to regulate emotions can be difficult not only for them but for those around them. If you notice that your loved one with BPD is on a high (despite their behavior suggesting otherwise), ask yourself whether their behavior is likely to cause harm to anyone else. If so, then you do need to step in and be honest about your concerns. While it's true that nobody likes to be told what to do, simply sharing your feelings with them and seeing how they feel may be the extra push they need to seek professional help.

How Common is a Full Recovery From BPD?

The good news is that BPD is not a lifelong sentence! With the right treatment and therapy, you can remove many, if not all, of the symptoms associated with this condition. With medication advancing and with the help of highly trained therapists, the percentage of people making a recovery from BPD is rising, with an impressive 88% of previously diagnosed patients no longer possessing symptoms that match the BPD criteria. This is why it is so important to seek professional help in the early stages of the disorder, before the symptoms create too many problems.

Chapter 2: Symptoms and Diagnosis

If you suspect that a loved one may have Borderline Personality Disorder, it's a really good idea to familiarize yourself with the diagnosis criteria before booking an appointment with your doctor. The Diagnostic and Statistical Manual of Mental Disorders (DSM) contains a list of criteria that each psychiatric disorder relates to. This can help the reader identify any matching symptoms. In this chapter, we'll be exploring these criteria in more detail, as well as understanding how and why these criteria were established.

How Is the Criteria Set and Assessed?

The criteria for BPD have been set by a team of medical professionals, including psychiatrists and psychologists. These criteria have been recorded in the DSM. The criteria are based on the best available research at the given time, but as research continues and improves, the criteria may also be adjusted. Every few years a new edition of the DSM is released with updated information based on new research, so it's important to keep yourself up to date on any important changes.

Assessment

Making an incorrect diagnosis can be very problematic for everyone involved, so it's absolutely vital that thorough and accurate assessments are conducted by a professional. Some of the key symptoms of BPD are related to a variety of other mental health disorders, so it can be easy to confuse them and make an incorrect diagnosis. Your doctor will usually conduct an interview with you where they ask you a variety of questions related to your symptoms, and they may also ask you to fill out a detailed questionnaire. Lastly, it is not uncommon for them to sit down with your loved ones to get a deeper understanding of your daily symptoms and challenges. All of this can help them to gain a more holistic view of your condition and make the most accurate diagnosis.

The Top Nine Symptoms

In an effort to make diagnosis easier and more clear-cut, professionals have grouped the top nine most common defining symptoms of BPD into categories. While these symptoms are certainly not the *only* ways in which the disorder manifests itself, they are the most commonly recognized. In order to be diagnosed, your symptoms need to match at least five out of the nine symptom categories that I am going to outline for you below. These symptoms also need to have been present for many years, stemming from the early adolescent phase. So, with all this in mind, let's jump straight into the top nine symptoms of BPD!

Extreme Mood Swings

Similar to those with depression or bipolar disorder, people with BPD are prone to intense mood swings. They can quickly go from feelings of euphoria to complete despondency, and they have very little control over these switches. One small trigger that would not upset the average person can send them off into a rollercoaster of uncontrollable emotions. What separates BPD from other disorders is the timeframe of these mood swings. For example, those with BPD tend to move on from their emotional switch after only a few minutes or a couple of hours, compared to the days or weeks seen in depression and bipolar disorder.

Emotional regulation is an ability that most people take for granted. However, those with BPD find it extremely difficult, to the point where it affects their jobs and relationships. I will go into deeper detail on this topic in later chapters of this book.

Impulsive Behavior and Self-Destruction

People with BPD have an intense urge to engage in dangerous, impulsive behaviors that ultimately end up causing themselves and others pain. Examples of impulsive behaviors include binge drinking, drugs, risky sexual encounters, driving under the influence, gambling, binge eating, or spending money excessively. Regardless of how it manifests itself, these behaviors are sensation-seeking and self-destructive, and only serve to help the person feel momentarily better.

Extreme Feelings of Anger

People with BPD have serious problems controlling their anger, and this can manifest itself outwardly or inwardly. Those with BPD may lash out at friends or family for no real reason, and this can be extremely upsetting. They may lose themselves in their anger by throwing things and screaming, unable to pull in the reins and regain their composure. Alternatively, they may direct their rage inwardly and spend the majority of their time feeling angry at themselves for no apparent reason. This, as you can imagine, can be extremely troubling to deal with.

Feelings of Suspicion and Dissociation

People with BPD regularly feel as if other people are judging or conspiring against them, even if that's far from the case. This is likely to cause increased feelings of paranoia and can create a disconnect between reality and their perception. When they feel as if they are under increased stress and pressure, they may start to dissociate from reality. This can be described as an out-of-body experience, where they quite literally feel as if they are living on a different plane and separate from their own being.

Feelings of Emptiness

People who suffer from BPD often report feeling empty inside, and they feel as if there is a large void within them that cannot be filled. Sadly, they struggle to pinpoint exactly what is missing in their lives, so they attempt to fill this emptiness with drugs, alcohol, food, or sex. The problem with this is that these feelings will continue indefinitely unless properly addressed, as nothing will truly leave them feeling happy and content, despite their best efforts.

Self-Harm

One of the more severe aspects of BPD is the act of self-harm and suicidal thoughts or tendencies. People with BPD are more prone to engaging in behaviors such as cutting, burning, or purging, and these behaviors are not only deliberate but extremely dangerous. Often, deliberate acts of self-harm can go horribly wrong, even if the individual doesn't intend to kill themselves, which is why they can be so devastating. On an even more concerning note, sufferers of BPD may attempt suicide. This usually begins with suicidal thoughts and threats, but it's very unpredictable.

Fear of Being Abandoned

People with BPD have an intense fear of being abandoned by the ones they care about the most. Most often this fear is completely unjustified, but it still feels extremely real and scary. They may feel triggered by a loved one meeting with a friend for dinner or going away for the weekend for a work function. Regardless of how innocent or short-lived the separation is, this feels very real for the individual and it ignites a fear that their loved one may never come back or wants to get away from them, even when this is far from the truth!

As a reaction to these feelings, they often act out by shouting, starting fights, clinging to them, or even threatening them. They may make attempts to stop the person from leaving and may try to track their movements while they are away. Constant phone calls are not uncommon either. Unfortunately, these behavioral patterns will only drive the person away. This can feel devastating for the individual with BPD and may be interpreted as justifying their fear of abandonment.

Disconnect with Self-Image

People who have BPD have a tendency to change jobs, sexual identity, religion, friends, lovers, and morals far more frequently than the average person. That said, there is a very good explanation for this! BPD individuals have a very tumultuous outlook on their self-image and tend to go from one extreme to the next. One moment they may feel confident and attractive, whereas the next they could feel as if they are totally worthless. They do not have a clear or accurate sense of self, and this makes it difficult for them to pinpoint what they want out of life. As a result of this, people with BDP very rarely have set goals to work towards, resulting in them feeling generally lost.

Rocky Relationships

As you can imagine, people with this disorder struggle to maintain healthy, lasting relationships with others and tend to drift more towards fleeting and passionate relationships. These relationships typically involve the other person being idolized and placed on a pedestal; the individual believes that this person alone can save them from their troubles. This, of course, dooms the relationship from the start and usually ends in tears and disappointment for both parties.

It is not uncommon for the individual to boast wildly about their love and affection for a new romantic interest, only to quickly sway to contempt and eventually hatred within months, weeks, or even days.

Always remember that the above symptoms are not reasoning alone to self-diagnose yourself with BPD. To get an accurate and reliable diagnosis, you need to visit your doctor and arrange an appointment with either a psychologist or psychiatrist.

Common Comorbidities

BPD is usually accompanied by additional conditions due to the nature of the disorder. It is not uncommon for a psychiatrist to make a dual diagnosis for people with BPD. These are some of the most common comorbidities:

- Anxiety disorders
- Eating disorders
- Bipolar disorder
- Depression

It is extremely important that any existing comorbidities are identified as soon as possible. If only part of the problem is being treated, it will be very difficult for the person to respond properly to the help they are receiving.

What Causes BPD?

At this point in time, researchers are still trying to understand the exact cause of BPD. Scientists believe that serotonin, the "happy" chemical located in your brain, is connected to the development of BPD. When this chemical is not being released as it should, this leaves the brain completely unable to regulate its mood.

Secondly, scientists believe that it is also the individual's environment that has a significant impact. Growing up in an abusive, unloving, and generally unstable home environment can play a significant role in developing BPD. Lastly, studies on twins have led researchers to believe that genetics also play a role in the development of BPD.

Since twins are genetically identical, their genes can be used to help researchers differentiate between the role of genetics versus environment when looking at the possible cause of a disorder. This means that you should check back on your family lineage if you are concerned that you may be at risk.

Who is Most at Risk?

While we do have an idea of some of the possible causes of BPD, there are certain groups of people who are more at risk than others. Typically, the people who are most likely to develop this disorder may have experienced:

- Child abuse
- Growing up around unstable or impulsive people
- Being emotionally unstable as a child
- Living with a family member with BPD

If you do suspect that you may have BPD, it's important to go to a medical professional and undergo a proper and accurate evaluation. Agreeing to more than one of the above statements certainly doesn't mean that you have the condition, so always seek out a professional opinion.

Chapter 3: Recognizing and Understanding the Triggers

In order to better understand a loved one with BPD and prevent any unwanted episodes, it's a good idea to try and understand the triggers behind their episodes. Almost every person who has BPD has certain triggers that can send their emotions into overdrive, and they may differ depending on the individual. That said, there are some very common triggers that ring true for many, so it's important to keep an eye out for these.

Essentially, a trigger can be described as an event that causes symptoms to soar out of control. This can be tied to an internal event such as a specific memory, or it can be an external event, such as someone raising their voice. For example, have you ever heard an old song that you and a loved one from your past used to listen to? The simple sound of this song can trigger some unexpected strong emotions that you have very little control over. The same idea applies to someone with BPD, except these triggers take place more frequently and the emotions can feel far more intense.

The Most Common Triggers

Mental Triggers

These are one of the most common types of triggers. These triggers don't necessarily have to be negative; it may be a positive memory that triggers the person to feel as if they are not as happy and content as they once were. Conversely, it can be a bad memory that acts as the trigger. This could be a traumatic event such as being bullied in school or abuse from a parent. This can set off some really intense emotions that can seriously offset BPD symptoms in the worst way.

Relationship Triggers

This ties back to the intense fear of being abandoned and rejected, and this can badly damage their self-esteem to the point of causing serious harm. They may turn to suicidal thoughts, self-harm, anger, or fear. They might lash out with hurtful words or compulsive, dangerous behaviors. Another term for this type of trigger is rejection sensitivity, and BPD sufferers are especially prone to this.

This can be triggered by something as small and insignificant as a sideways glance from a colleague or a phone call that is not picked up by a friend. While most people would simply assume that the person is busy, someone with BPD would overthink to the point where they feel that they are unwanted by their friend or are being ignored. This can quickly spiral into intrusive thoughts that their friend hates them and doesn't want to associate with them anymore. The vast majority of the time this is completely untrue, but they don't see it that way!

Identifying Individual Triggers

While it's easy to look at generic triggers, every individual will have their own set of personal triggers that they need to identify and understand. By doing this, you are better preparing yourself for these types of situations and can hopefully prevent an episode altogether. You also find that these triggers don't simply come from nowhere, but instead are a result of unresolved traumas. That said, it's time to dig deeper to discover these triggers so that you can work on developing effective coping mechanisms!

If you or your loved one is feeling ready, then you can practice the below exercise to help you identify your triggers and find a way to get through them.

Prepare

For this first step, it's imperative that you are in a relatively healthy headspace. If you're feeling fragile and emotional, wait until you've cleared things up. If you're confident and ready to tackle your issues, then grab a pen and a notebook and get started! Find a quiet, calm spot in your home where you can be alone with your thoughts and won't be disturbed, then get comfortable.

Draw Up Columns

Next, you're going to draw up three columns, with each column stating a different heading. The first heading should be the "trigger", the second "emotions/feelings", and the third heading should be "my response to this feeling or emotion".

Recall an Emotional Situation

For this next part, you'll have to be strong and bring yourself to recall a triggering event when you had a deeply negative and emotional response to a specific situation. Perhaps your parents got a divorce, or you experienced a traumatic incident during childhood. Remember that this doesn't only have to be a response to something that was done to you, it can also be an internal emotion such as shame, loneliness, or emptiness.

Regardless of where the trigger came from, you need to find the strength to recall and acknowledge that it happened, so that you can move on to the next stage.

Explore and Pinpoint Your Emotions

For this next step, you'll need to try your best to identify how you felt. What was your response to this trigger? While this isn't always an easy thing to do, you want to try and identify this as accurately as possible. You may have felt anxious, jealous, angry, alone, or simply sad. Whichever emotion it was, be sure to jot it down. If you felt more than one, make sure that you write all of them down under the "emotions/feelings" column. Remember to take your time and don't rush!

How You Responded

For the next column, you'll need to think about how you responded to these emotions. Did you binge eat a whole lot of food shortly after the incident, or did you find yourself heading straight to the bar for an episode of binge drinking? Did you turn to drugs? Whatever your response was, try your best to accurately recall it and jot it down. Again, it can be more than one response!

Remember that your response doesn't necessarily have to be a negative one. Perhaps you responded well to the trigger.

Repeat

Follow the above steps for at least two to three more memories and fill the columns in. Try and do as many accurate memories as you possibly can! If you can only remember a few, that's okay.

Search for Patterns

Next, you're going to pay particular attention to the column that says "triggers", as this is what you want to try and understand.

Do you see any patterns as you look at your list of triggers? Perhaps there are certain people in your life that repeatedly show up, or certain locations. Are you repeatedly triggered in large, open spaces with lots of people, or do situations when you're completely alone trigger negative emotions? Regardless of the pattern, see if you can identify them. Make a note of this!

Try to put these emotions into specific categories. For example, "sadness and emptiness when alone for long periods of time" could be a common emotion and situation that you can categorize.

Keep Tabs

Going forward, don't simply move on and forget about your list! Make an effort to continuously monitor and add any new emotions or triggers to the columns. Be sure to reflect on the situation, the emotions you felt, and your response to how this made you feel. Now, take a look again at your list and see if you can pick up on any new patterns. Be sure to make note of everything, including the smaller details!

Anticipate and Communicate

Now that you have a clearer understanding of your triggers, reactions, and common patterns of them combined, it should be much easier to foretell a triggering situation and avoid it. Once you have this ability, you'll find that you'll have an easier time avoiding triggering situations and preventing any unnecessary emotional spirals. You'll also have a great reference for your triggers when developing appropriate coping strategies, which is also a huge step forward.

Once you feel ready, you should share your trigger patterns with a loved one or a professional. Your therapist will be able to help you develop strategies for handling these triggering situations on a professional level, meaning you will be well-equipped moving forward.

How to Avoid Triggers

Now that you know what your triggers are, you're probably wondering where to go from here? It may sound like the obvious answer is to simply evade your triggers like the plague, but avoiding them altogether isn't always the easiest and most realistic option! That said, there are some situations that you can avoid simply by making the effort to plan your schedule around them or simply choosing not to engage in certain activities.

For example, if a certain family member or friend is a common trigger for you, you can stop making plans with them or cancel any upcoming commitments. This may be easier if they are a close friend. Sometimes it can be trickier to get distance from family members, especially if you live with them. In situations like this, avoidance isn't necessarily the answer. If you are able to stay away from certain locations that trigger you, then do so. However, if the location or person that triggers you is your workplace and boss, you're going to have a really tough time avoiding that (unless you quit, which isn't always realistic)!

Often, avoiding all your triggers completely is simply not possible, so you'll need to devise alternative strategies for coping. This is especially important if the situation makes up an important part of your life. While it may seem like the easier option to run away from them, it's not always realistic or healthy. In this case, you'll need to sit down with your therapist and talk about developing a trigger action plan that you can follow to get through these situations.

Chapter 4: Treatment for Borderline Personality Disorder

As with everything in life, there is always a silver lining if you look for it! Fortunately, there are several promising treatment options for BPD that you can choose from. BPD is usually treated with a combination of therapy and medications, but the styles of treatment and types of medication can vary. In this chapter, you will be learning about all the different treatment options that your doctor will suggest to you.

Medications

Firstly, I'll start off with some of the medication options that doctors typically prescribe for treatment. Medications can be especially beneficial for the treatment of depression and anxiety symptoms that are often present with BPD. It is important to know that there is no specific, FDA-approved medication that is specifically designed for the treatment of BPD, but rather, there are certain ones that seem to help with many of the symptoms associated with it.

Why Should I Give Medications a Try?

Many people are skeptical when it comes to going on medications, especially for the first time. Sometimes the dosage isn't quite right, or they react badly to the medication, and this can put people off. That said, with some trial and error and perseverance you can find just the right one for you, and this can dramatically change your quality of life! Making the decision to find the right medications to manage your condition is a responsible decision that will improve your work and personal relationships.

Taking medications can also help manage specific symptoms such as anxiety, mood swings, depression, and paranoia. Tackling these symptoms head-on is an excellent way to ensure that they are not only managed but also that they will not worsen over time. Ensuring that you take your medications regularly will also safeguard you from suicidal thoughts and actions that may accompany BPD. Lastly, taking medications will also help to minimize and prevent any co-occurring disorders that commonly exist alongside BPD. These include bipolar disorder, eating disorders, substance use disorders, depression, and anxiety.

Common Medications

Antipsychotics

Antipsychotic drugs are commonly used to treat anger problems associated with BPD. While they have been shown to assist with anger and impulsivity, they appear to have some serious side effects that are difficult to ignore. This is why many doctors only prescribe them in really severe cases, as they may worsen other BPD symptoms over time. One of the most concerning effects of antipsychotics over the long term is severe involuntary tremors that may never go away. If antipsychotics are required, the patient should be carefully monitored throughout the process. Some of the most common antipsychotics are Loxitane, Prolixin Decanoate, Navane, and Haldol.

Each one has their own specific set of symptoms that they target which a doctor will analyze and prescribe accordingly.

Mood Stabilizers

As the name suggests, mood stabilizers (or anticonvulsants) are commonly prescribed to treat symptoms of BPD. In particular, these medications target the impulsivity and mood swings that are so frequent when it comes to BPD. Some of the most common mood stabilizers are Lamictal, Lithobid, Tegretol, and Depakote.

One of the more common mood stabilizers, Lithobid, can cause the following side effects:

- Weight gain
- Dizziness and fatigue
- Acne
- Vomiting and nausea
- Tremors
- Thyroid and kidney complications

In general, every type of anticonvulsant comes with its own set of side effects that are similar to Lithobid, with weight gain, fatigue, and rashes being the most commonly reported. Your doctor will go through all of these with you and advise you to report back if the side effects become too severe. They will also do any relevant tests to ensure that your body is functioning properly while on the medication.

Antidepressants

Antidepressants are commonly prescribed for people who suffer from chronic depression; they work by altering the chemicals in the brain in favor of a happier, brighter mood. In fact, various studies worldwide have found that 80% of patients with BPD are prescribed antidepressants. Since low mood is one of the more common symptoms of BPD, it may be a good idea to try out an antidepressant to counteract some of these symptoms. That said, there are many antidepressants available on the market, with varying strengths and side effects. The tricky part is finding one that works best for you, which may happen straight away or through some trial and error!

Antidepressants are split into two main categories, and these are selective serotonin reuptake inhibitors (SSRIs) and monoamine oxidase inhibitors (MAOIs). The difference between the two is that MAOIs work by blocking out certain chemicals in the brain, and SSRIs focus primarily on helping the brain to produce more serotonin (the happy chemical in the brain). When it comes to preference, SSRIs tend to be the most commonly used form of antidepressant as they are usually more effective and appear to have fewer side effects.

That said, there are still some side effects associated with SSRIs, but they are not as harsh as their counterparts, and are usually short-lived and modest in their severity. The most commonly prescribed SSRIs are Paxil, Prozac, and Luvox.

Each of them has slightly different effects, but your doctor will prescribe them according to your specific symptoms.

Anxiolytics/Anti-anxiety

Anti-anxiety medications are commonly prescribed for the treatment of serious anxiety in BPD patients. Anxiety is an exceptionally common symptom for people with BPD, and their anxiety is not like most others. Yes, we all experience some anxiousness from day to day if we have a big project or event coming up—but this does not compare to how someone with BPD experiences it! Prolonged anxiety that lasts for several hours and even days can be extremely debilitating, which is why it is vital that treatment is provided as soon as possible.

Anti-anxiety medications work by prompting the brain to release more Gamma-aminobutyric acid (GABA), which helps to calm the brain down and be less receptive to distress. When it comes to these medications, fatigue and mental fogginess are not uncommon, which can be problematic. One other concern is that you cannot stop anti-anxiety medications straight away if they aren't working for you. This can result in some serious withdrawal symptoms such as seizures, increased heart rate, tremors, dizziness, and nausea. You should always consult with your doctor before considering stopping so that you can be weaned off them gradually. The most common anti-anxiety medications are Valium, Xanax, Klonopin, and Ativan.

It may feel very overwhelming with all the available medications, but remember that your doctor will work with you to find the right ones for you. Some people are very lucky and manage to find the correct medication quickly, whereas others have to try a few before they find the right fit. Regardless, it's certainly worth the effort!

Top Psychotherapy Options

Psychotherapy is very commonly used in conjunction with medication to effectively treat BPD. While medication is important for regulating the chemicals in the brain, psychotherapy is vital for a variety of reasons. Psychotherapy provides the patient with the mental tools to cope with the symptoms of BPD without relying solely on medication. It also helps the patient to be more aware of the emotions of those around them and helps them to control impulsivity and anger.

Dialectical Behavior Therapy (DBT)

This first method of treatment was initially designed solely for the purpose of BPD, but due to its effectiveness, has now become a common treatment for a variety of other conditions such as eating disorders and substance abuse. DBT is a form of cognitive-behavioral therapy, meaning that its main focus is to change the way the patient thinks so that they develop healthier thought patterns. The aim is for them to learn how to cope better in stressful situations, manage their emotions, and have healthy relationships with those around them.

DBT can take many different forms and is usually broken up into three types of therapy: group, individual, and phone coaching. Depending on the patient's preference and needs, they can choose to see a therapist face-to-face, or engage in a group with a trained therapist to learn how to manage their emotions. They can also phone their therapist for advice if they feel they are in a situation that they cannot control and need professional guidance. As an evidence-based psychotherapy approach, DBT is broken up into a variety of different techniques, which I will list and explain below.

Tolerance to Distress

This first technique is vital for the treatment of BPD as it helps the patient learn how to cope effectively with distressing situations. Instead of losing control, distress tolerance will help you to remain calm in any situation by utilizing four key techniques. These techniques are distraction, self-soothing, improving the moment, and comparing the pros and cons of controlling your emotions versus losing your cool and creating drama. The key here is to learn the ability of distraction in order to allow yourself more time to think before you react.

A good example of a common tolerance to distress exercise is advising the patient to engage in an activity that allows their emotions to follow their body. This could be going for a walk outside, playing an instrument, or writing your feelings down.

Emotion Regulation

Emotion regulation is a vital skill that enables you to manage your emotions so that they do not take over your thoughts and actions completely. This is achieved through identifying and naming your feelings so that you can better understand and change them into something more positive. Essentially, the aim here is to direct negative emotions into more positive ones, which can only be done by identifying the emotions you are feeling.

For example, if you are feeling hurt or frustrated by your partner's actions, you may want to distance yourself and avoid them completely. By regulating your emotions, you can teach yourself to instead spend time with them and communicate so that you can resolve the conflict and build a healthy relationship.

Interpersonal Effectiveness

This next method is key to helping the patient keep and establish healthy boundaries within a relationship without damaging said relationship. This technique gives the patient the tools to say "no" by practicing effective communication, learning respect for themselves and others, and learning to deal with difficult people. This is split into what is known as the GIVE steps, which are listed below:

- **G**entle: Avoid aggression and attacking the other person when expressing an opinion.
- **I**nterest: Use effective listening by allowing the other person to speak and listening to what they have to say.
- **V**alidate: Show the other person that you acknowledge their thoughts and feelings.
- **E**asy: Show the person that you are firm yet lighthearted by smiling and remaining positive.

Mindfulness

Mindfulness is another key approach used in DBT as it helps the patient learn to live in the moment and acknowledge their surroundings. Mindfulness helps you to be more aware of your senses, impulses, and emotions in a positive and non-judgmental manner. By slowing things down and living in the present, you are enabling yourself to cope with difficult situations and emotions in a calm and sensible fashion. Mindfulness prevents any emotional or aggressive outbursts, which are common in patients with BPD.

When it comes to practicing mindfulness, breathing exercises are a common start. For example, many mindfulness exercises involve paying attention to each breath that you inhale and exhale. You should be mindful of how it feels, and the motion of your chest rising and falling. The same can be applied to eating, and this is why mindfulness is also commonly used to treat various eating disorders, as it teaches the patient to focus on the taste and experience of enjoying the food rather than using the food as a form of escapism.

Mentalization-Based Therapy (MBT)

MBT therapy is yet another evidence-based approach that uses a combination of both modern and older psychoanalytic approaches to treat BPD. Essentially, mentalization refers to talking to yourself in such a way that you understand and acknowledge your thoughts and feelings in a healthy manner, therefore creating a stable sense of self. Experts believe that MBT is effective for BPD as it involves very basic training and tackles the key problems related to BPD; this is primarily the inability to manage and understand emotions. People with BPD often feel overwhelmed and unable to cope with their emotions, which can often lead to self-destructive behaviors. MBT tackles this by giving them the tools to identify and manage these emotions, therefore preventing an emotional outburst or damaging behaviors.

Treatment is typically long-term for MBT and can last anywhere between one year to 18 months. Therapy sessions involve openly discussing what is going on in your life, including any difficulties or traumatic events. That said, the patient is also encouraged to discuss family members and close friends, as their actions and thoughts also have an impact. The aim is for the patient to recognize and understand their own emotions as well as others, thus enabling them to better handle their impulses and reactions in a stressful situation.

Schema-Focused Therapy

The main idea behind schema-focused therapy is that childhood traumas have a direct impact on how we perceive the world around us. When basic childhood needs such as love and acceptance are not met, maladaptive early schemas are developed. In other words, the individual is unable to process and understand emotions, meaning they respond in unhealthy ways. The schema theory supports the fact that the symptoms of BPD are often a result of traumatic childhood experiences, which means that schema-focused therapy is one of the best ways to treat these symptoms.

Schemas can be described as general patterns of thought and behavior that ultimately determine how we view the world and the way in which we react to certain situations. Things can go wrong when childhood schemas are warped due to stressful or traumatic situations, and this can trigger a trauma response if a similar situation presents itself in adult life. Essentially, the development of unhealthy or toxic schemas in childhood tends to carry through to adulthood. The focus of schema therapy is to tackle and rectify these issues so that they no longer create an unhealthy trigger response.

By now you're probably wondering what these unhealthy schemas may look like in someone with BPD. Well, people with BPD often have an intense fear of abandonment, meaning that they are terrified of their loved ones leaving them. As a consequence, they may leave people they care about in an attempt to leave before they themselves are left. They may also engage in relationships where they are treated unfairly as this is how they were raised to be treated. Alternatively, they may hold onto loved ones too tightly, which is known as enmeshment. This means that they feel they cannot be content or successful without a loved one, so they become too dependent on others. On the opposite end of the spectrum, they may isolate themselves from the world around them as they feel as if they do not fit in. At the end of the day, the schema depends entirely on the past experiences of the individual.

Every individual responds to childhood schemas differently, and these can be defined as three separate methods of coping:

1. Overcompensation: This refers to the individual behaving in an extreme manner when exposed to a situation that reminds them of an early schema, thus they engage in behaviors that are the extreme opposite of this schema.

2. Surrender: This means that the individual behaves in a way that reinforces their childhood schemas.

3. Avoidance: This means that the person deliberately goes out of their way to avoid situations that trigger feelings of stress, anxiety, and vulnerability.

Once a therapist has identified which category their patient fits into, they can conduct therapy accordingly. Schema-focused therapy has been shown to be effective for BPD patients and should be practiced in conjunction with medication prescribed by a professional.

Transference-Focused Therapy

What separates this type of therapy from others is the fact that the therapist focuses on concerning behaviors that arise during the therapy session rather than outside of it. The key aim is to help the individual develop healthier ways to cope with self-destructive behaviors by improving their self-esteem. This idea focuses on the meaning of transference, which essentially means the projection of one's emotions and feelings onto another. The person usually isn't aware that this is happening, so they subconsciously project their feelings of fear or anger onto an unsuspecting person as a coping method.

As you may already be thinking, this certainly isn't the healthiest way to deal with your thoughts and emotions! With this in mind, a therapist will assume that transference will take place between the patient and the therapist, and they will try to unpackage the meaning behind this occurrence. The therapist will achieve this by asking the patient to identify examples of transferability in the therapy session, and then they can uncover how the patient can better handle this outside of the therapy room.

This therapy works using the object relations theory which emphasizes the fact that humans relate better to social connections rather than aggression or sex. Essentially, the patients are taught that this is how each person wants to connect and encourages open communication upon this basis. The main goal is to help ease symptoms such as impulsivity, aggression, suicidal thoughts, anxiety, and self-harm. The therapist will need to develop a trusting bond between themselves and the patient, as the patient will need to truly open up to the therapist so that they can take responsibility for their actions and make the necessary changes. In other words, they need to stop blaming their diagnosis for their behavior and take responsibility for their treatment by doing what needs to be done.

Tips for Getting the Most Out of Therapy

While therapy can be incredibly beneficial for the improvement of BPD symptoms and a healthier outlook on life, it can be intimidating at first. If you truly want to see positive changes, you need to be fully committed and engaged in your therapy sessions. Without positivity and commitment, you or your loved ones are wasting precious time and money, which isn't fair to anyone. With this in mind, I'm going to run through some effective tips you can follow to get the most out of therapy.

Surround Yourself with Support

Before you begin any type of therapy, make sure that you have a strong support system that you can rely on. It can be easy to self-isolate when feeling overwhelmed or judged, and this can be highly detrimental to progress. If you don't have a friend or family member to provide you with the support you need, you may benefit greatly from a BPD support group. You will be able to chat openly with other individuals who are going through similar struggles, and this can be a good way to practice open communication before you begin with therapy.

Actively Engage in Your Treatment

You can have the best therapist in the world with an incredible support structure, but without your personal engagement, you won't see much progress. In order to grow and move past your troubles, you need to be actively engaged and present in your therapy sessions. As difficult as it may be, honesty and transparency with your therapist is the best way to achieve meaningful progress and establish rapport. Ask as many questions as you can and never be afraid to research things before your therapy session so that you can have questions prepared.

Secondly, never be afraid to change your treatment plan if you feel that it isn't working for you. With so many available methods of treatment, you're bound to find one that works well for you.

Ensure That You Have a Safety Plan

The journey through therapy can be both rewarding and challenging, and it's often filled with difficult emotions. Sometimes these emotions are manageable, whereas other times they can be truly overwhelming and result in dangerous thoughts and impulses. In order to prevent these from coming to fruition, draw up an emergency contingency plan that you can rely on.

The idea behind this is to have a plan you can utilize when things go wrong, and you feel alone; this may even save your life. When you are in a good place mentally, draw up a plan you can follow if you're feeling impulsive and are wanting to self-harm. This can be kept aside for when you are feeling scared or in a harmful situation and may save you from making a bad decision.

Taking Care of Your Body

While it's incredibly important to take good care of your mental health, your physical health is also a vital aspect. Eating a healthy, balanced diet and following a regular exercise routine will help you to feel better physically and mentally. Taking care of your body is good for your confidence and self-esteem, which directly impacts your mood and self-awareness. You also need to make sure that you are getting plenty of quality sleep by maintaining a regular sleep schedule. Lastly, make time for activities that relax you and bring joy to your life, as this is an excellent way to keep stress at bay.

Once you get yourself in a good routine, you'll find it much easier to manage your BPD symptoms and engage fully with therapy.

Chapter 5: Techniques for Helping a Loved One

If you are reading this book because you have a loved one with BPD, you'll already know how emotionally and mentally taxing it can be. You love the person deeply, yet somehow you feel helpless in the face of their condition. If you can relate, know that you are certainly not alone! Living with someone with BPD can mean days of emotional turmoil, with the sufferer under immense emotional distress. When these days come, you'll need to arm yourself with the tools to be the best support structure you can possibly be, which is exactly what you will learn about in this chapter.

Best Strategies for Coping

Establish Rapport Through Confidence and Respect

As you know by now, people with BPD typically have a history of childhood trauma. This means that they can have a distrustful outlook on others and the world in general, leaving them feeling vulnerable and unsafe. As a loved one in their life, it is your job to do your best to instill a sense of safety and confidence within them. Show them that you have confidence in their ability to succeed and be the best possible version of themselves. While it may be tempting to make decisions for them, you're better off guiding them in the right direction, and then ultimately allowing them to make the final call.

Always be willing to offer help and advice, but only when they ask for it. Convey to them your willingness to always offer a helping hand or to be there to listen, but never be too pushy. Once your loved ones feel that they can take comfort in your understanding and knowledge, they will feel more able to take on other challenges on their own.

Encourage and Identify Strengths

Individuals with BPD usually have a fractured sense of self and identity, meaning that they're generally unsure of what makes them unique. They have a warped idea of how other people see them, and this only adds to their anxiety. That said, helping them to identify their key strengths is an excellent way to help boost their confidence and develop a better understanding of who they are. You can do this by identifying and remembering situations where they demonstrated a positive strength or attribute. Recall this moment with them and encourage them to repeat this behavior and remind them of why they did a good job.

That said, always make sure that you are completely honest with them in this regard. While the aim here is to boost their confidence, you want to make sure you're doing it to genuinely help them and not provide false hope.

Educate Yourself

One of the most important things you can do for a loved one with BPD is to educate yourself about the disorder. That said, the fact that you're reading this book means you're already halfway there, so well done! To add to this, it's important for you to fully understand BPD so that you can respond in the best possible way. Remember, it is your responsibility to avoid adding fuel to the fire, especially when your loved one is experiencing a severe emotional episode. By responding in a calm and helpful manner, you'll be more likely to diffuse the situation and provide a sense of calm.

For example, someone with BPD can see a completely normal situation as an argument-provoking opportunity. A canceled coffee date for a legitimate reason may lead them to believe that they are being abandoned or rejected, and this may lead them to lash out. Instead of simply rescheduling the appointment, the BPD individual may completely avoid future interaction or demand to be seen immediately. Regardless of the outcome, the BPD sufferer can respond with an intense emotional reaction that can drive others away. The best way to handle this is to understand that they are simply responding as a result of fear and not hatred, and you need to do your best to convey understanding. Remember, they're simply feeling misunderstood and are looking for some comfort and understanding from someone they care about.

Be a Source of Trust

As you know, people with BPD usually have a tumultuous past when it comes to trust. As children, they may have grown up in a household where they felt they had nobody they could turn to for trustworthy advice. In fact, they may have had their trust shattered multiple times! This is where you can be their beacon of hope—demonstrate to them that they can confide in you with complete confidentiality. Unless what they share with you could cause harm to them or others, keep what they tell you to yourself to build a foundation of trust and honesty. Do your best to follow through with your promises and avoid letting them down at the last minute.

That said, don't make promises that you cannot keep. Rather, set limits that are realistic and fit into your schedule so that you can be there when you say you will and establish a relationship of trust.

Encourage Professional Assistance

It can be extremely daunting for any person to seek professional help, especially when it can uncover darker aspects of themselves that they aren't ready to discover. This rings especially true for someone with BPD, despite the fact that therapy can help them to tackle their anxiety and depression. You can step in by encouraging them to take this brave leap and providing them with information on the way forward. You can also go as far as assisting them in booking their first appointment, if they feel comfortable with you doing so.

Group and individual therapy can be incredibly effective at managing BPD symptoms, especially if the person is suffering from depression, anxiety, or engaging in self-harm. The opportunity to speak about it with a professional can really help them to open up and explore alternative ways to manage their intense emotions.

Keep a Close Watch for Suicidal Tendencies

People with BPD have a much higher chance of committing suicide than the general population, meaning that you'll need to take this extra seriously. If they ever bring it up with you or give any signals that indicate it, then you need to have a serious conversation with them. Be transparent with them by expressing your concerns and intentions to take action if you feel they are a danger to themselves. Never be afraid to contact a professional or a suicide helpline if you feel that your loved one is in serious trouble!

If it is a false alarm, they may be angry or embarrassed. However, it's better to be safe than sorry, so always take extra precautions to ensure their safety if you feel the need.

Handle Conflict Using Attachment

For someone with BPD, conflict really can be a make-or-break moment (even when it doesn't have to be). Conflict is a perfectly normal part of any relationship and can even make a relationship stronger if handled properly. That said, someone with BPD does not view it this way—in fact, conflict is seen as a marker for abandonment and rejection, resulting in feelings of shame and guilt. A small conflict may even prompt someone with BPD to question the entire relationship; this can be damaging for both parties. As a support structure, it is up to you to encourage them to view conflicts as building blocks to a stronger relationship.

If and when conflicts arise between yourself and a loved one, take care to continue to build the relationship and push through those difficulties. By remaining caring and attached throughout conflicts, you're healing the BPD individual and encouraging meaningful and lasting change. If a conflict arises and you're not sure how to handle it, try and focus on that specific behavior rather than making them feel as if you are attacking their character. Arrange a phone call or a visit to discuss the conflict and a way forward, and assure them that while you're unhappy with what happened, you're here to stay and won't give up on them.

Practice Self-Awareness

This one is extremely important as it involves your own self-care and boundaries. Making the effort to understand and support a loved one with BPD is an incredible thing to do for several reasons. That said, it can also be extremely emotionally draining when you allow yourself to give more than you take in a relationship. Pay careful attention to your stress levels and understand your limits. Always express how you feel in the kindest manner and explain that you need to look after yourself so that you can be the best possible support structure.

Always bear in mind that every healthy relationship requires give and take, but a relationship with someone with BPD requires a little bit more giving on your side. Never be afraid to express when you need a little break, but emphasize that this is not the end of the relationship.

Make Time for Enjoyable Activities

One of the best ways that you can build rapport and bond with a loved one with one BPD is by arranging soothing and enjoyable activities together. Make sure that the activity you choose is mutually enjoyed and encourages relaxation and fun. Activities such as hiking, walking, the movies, coffee, or lunch are all healthy outings that will encourage positive interactions and strengthen your bond. Not only will you enjoy yourself and feel more relaxed, but your loved one with BPD will feel more securely attached. Try and schedule these outings at least once per week and do your best to honor your commitment to the plans!

Chapter 6: Setting Healthy Boundaries and Communication

In the previous chapters, we discussed how incredibly important it is to not only be there for your loved one with BPD but also to take care of your own needs. While this was only touched on briefly, this chapter will dive into deeper detail on how you can best communicate with and set healthy boundaries with someone with BPD. The key to maintaining a healthy relationship for both parties is understanding how to communicate effectively, which is exactly what will be covered in this chapter. Let's get started!

Why Are Boundaries So Important?

Individuals with BPD tend to take their anger out on the people closest to them, which can be extremely traumatic and emotionally draining for their loved ones. Having to cope with this continuously can leave the person feeling completely at a loss, as this can feel like abuse. At times this may feel as if you are powerless, and the BPD symptoms have taken over complete control. While this may seem true, the truth is that you have more control than you think!

No matter who it is that has BPD, you owe it to them and yourself to learn new techniques for dealing with these problems. This will help you to communicate better and improve your relationship with them, even if you feel that it is one-sided. By taking control over your own reactions, establishing calm and clear communication, and setting limits, you can speed up signs of improvement and provide a clear example as to how two people should interact with calmness and respect.

By now you likely already know that a loved one has BPD, so you know the signs and symptoms to watch out for. If you're not sure, you can refer back to the second chapter. For now, you need to prioritize your own needs and mental health so that you can be the best possible support structure for them, which brings me to my next point.

Important Steps to Self-Care

If you are a parent of a child with BPD, it can be extremely easy to slip into a pattern of pandering to their every whim in the hopes that you can evade an outburst. In all honesty, you're not doing yourself or your child any favors by doing this. In fact, doing this will only result in burnout on your side and possibly depression and additional mental health problems. Plus, your child likely won't come knocking on your door to thank you for your sacrifices! So, what's the best way forward?

The best thing you can do for a loved one with BPD is put on your own set of armor before entering the battlefield. If you don't, you'll end up getting shot down and losing the battle! In order to do this, you might like to try the steps listed below.

Join Your Own BPD Support Group

Firstly, you need to remember that you are certainly not alone in this! There are plenty of other people out in the world that are going through the same hardships, and it can definitely help you to feel better if you can relate with others. Check your local paper if there are any support groups in the area, or alternatively, you can join an online BPD forum. What matters is that you can share your experience and feelings with others and stand to gain some useful advice. At the very least, you'll have a safe space to vent!

Keep Others Close

When you are dealing with a difficult case of BPD, it can be very easy to distance yourself from other people in the hopes that they won't fall victim or witness to an aggressive outburst. The problem with this is that you are isolating yourself from friends and family who care about you and may even want to help. As a human being, you need a helping hand, a shoulder to lean on, and someone that will listen to your concerns and give you a realistic response. By isolating yourself, you're opening yourself up to manipulation from the BPD individual, which is not healthy for either of you.

Watch Stress Levels

It can be extremely tempting to lose your cool when you've had a long day at work and your emotions are running high. That said, if you lose your temper and the BPD person follows suit, you're looking at a potentially massive blowout. You also need to know that the individual will often test your patience, and an angry, hostile response will only fuel their anger. To avoid this, do what you can to manage your stress levels, whether it's slow breathing, yoga, meditation, or exercise. Deep breathing techniques are one of the best ways to curb anxiety and stress as it happens.

Prioritize Your Health

It can be extremely easy to neglect your diet, sleep, and exercise routine when you're in the middle of an emotionally tumultuous week. As much as you don't feel like it, this is a time when you should be prioritizing these things. If you're sleep-deprived and eating poorly, you're definitely not going to be in any fit state to properly handle a BPD sufferer's symptoms in the most effective manner. Make sure you are eating plenty of whole foods, drinking enough water, exercising a few times per week, and getting at least seven to eight hours of sleep every night. This will help you to better control your own emotions and stress.

Make Time for Yourself (and Others)

While it can be very time-consuming having a BPD person in your life, this doesn't mean that they should take up all your time! Allowing yourself to have a life outside your relationship with them is not only good for you, but for them too. You'll feel more refreshed once you've had some time out with others, and you'll gain a renewed outlook on the situation. This can only benefit your relationship with them, and you'll feel much calmer and relaxed as a result.

Communicating Effectively

While we have touched briefly on the best ways to approach some common scenarios with a BPD person, now we'll be focusing on some core communication skills that you'll need to harness in future situations. Once you have a plan as to how you will react in an outburst, you'll be able to diffuse the situation much faster. With this in mind, here are a few effective ways that you can improve communication, prevent outbursts, and improve your relationship.

Focus More on Feelings Than What is Said

An individual with BPD sometimes finds it difficult to express how they truly feel, and this results in their words being misconstrued. As a result, their intentions and emotions are misunderstood, which only makes them feel more isolated. What you can do to help is try and focus on the emotions behind the words that they say—perhaps their words come out as aggressive, but they're really just sad. One of the biggest needs that BPD people have is to feel acknowledged, so you need to dig a little bit deeper to understand what their words truly mean.

Next time your loved one lashes out, ask them questions and try to move past their words to the underlying emotion they are feeling. Instead of throwing their words back at them, try expressing that you understand how they feel and that you're willing to listen.

Don't Bring Them Down (Listen)

As I mentioned in the point above, try your best to put aside your ego, even when the person is really testing your patience. Even if they are being completely irrational, you need to find it within yourself to rise above it and remain calm and collected. It's totally normal to feel the urge to try and win the argument or tell them they're completely wrong. It's only human nature! What you need to do instead is to hear them out and show them that despite the fact that you don't always agree with them, you're willing to hear what they have to say.

Identify the Right Time for a Conversation

Even if you really need to have a conversation and get something off your chest, make absolutely sure that you've chosen an appropriate opportunity. If your loved one is threatening you, raising their voice, and are just angry in general, now is *certainly* not the time! The best thing you can do is express to them that you do want to have a chat, but at a later stage once they have cooled down. If need be, remove yourself from the situation and approach them again once the storm has settled.

Don't Focus Solely on Their Disorder

While the disorder may feel as if it takes prominence in your life, it's important not to convey that to your loved one. Do your best to talk about subjects other than BPD to lighten the mood and show your loved ones that your lives do not revolve solely around their condition. Take the time to show interest in their life and their activities, and always openly encourage the positives.

Distraction is Key

If you can sense your loved one is upset and on the brink of an outburst, do your best to distract them with an activity or something that they enjoy. Whether it's bringing up an old memory, the suggestion of a walk or trip to the shops, or a cup of their favorite tea, make sure that you distract them! All your loved one needs right now is something that will calm and soothe them as quickly as possible, and it's up to you to initiate this in order to prevent an episode.

Practice Sympathy and Active Listening

As you may have already experienced, conversing with someone with BPD can sometimes feel like talking to a young child. While it can be tempting to brush them aside or respond with an equally immature remark, the best thing you can do is focus your full attention on them without distraction from the TV or your phone. Avoid redirecting the discussion to your own issues and instead, try to keep the focus on what they are trying to convey. Even if you don't agree with what they are saying, avoid criticism and blame at all costs—it will get you *nowhere*!

The Key Steps to Setting Healthy Boundaries

There's no easy way to tell someone with BPD that you have to lay your boundaries out in order to preserve the relationship, especially when they are so sensitive. While it may be difficult at first, learning how to set your boundaries and stick with them will benefit both of you in the long term! Here you will learn how to set your boundaries, explain them kindly to your loved one with BPD, and most importantly, maintain them.

Preparation Stage

Decide on Your Boundaries

Congratulations! You have now made the decision to lay out some personal boundaries between yourself and your loved one—you're already halfway there! When it comes to boundary setting, some people get a little bit confused as to how exactly they should determine and set them. To make things easier, your boundaries are essentially a reflection of your values and morals. Once you know these, you can protect yourself from situations that will make you feel uncomfortable.

For example, let's say one of your core values is honesty and integrity. If you have a person in your life that is constantly lying, it's going to cause a massive rift in your relationship and hurt you deeply. If your loved one lies to you on a regular basis, you need to let them know that this is unacceptable, and you will not tolerate it. Express to them clearly that this is a dealbreaker for you, and if they can't respect that then you'll need some serious space.

Regardless, make a list of all your boundaries ahead of time and possible examples of what crossing them may look like. It's also useful to recall past experiences of when these boundaries were crossed for reference.

Decide on a Plan

Most importantly, you need to decide on a plan as to how you will react if these boundaries are crossed. If you don't, you may not be equipped to handle the situation in the moment, and your reaction may not be adequate. Remember, the key to setting boundaries is to gain respect, so make sure that your reaction to their behavior mirrors this sentiment.

For example, if your loved one raises their voice and swears at you, you need to respond appropriately. Now, you've had your discussion about your negative feelings towards shouting and expletives, yet your loved one has still crossed the boundary. Instead of shouting back at them, a good idea is to remove yourself from the situation completely. Leave the house for a few hours if you need to, and allow them time alone to think about the gravity of their behavior.

Make sure that you have already planned this before the event occurs so that you know your action plan beforehand.

Prepare for Backlash

People with BPD tend to be overly sensitive to changes in other peoples' behavior, especially those they care about. With this in mind, it's not uncommon for them to react with embarrassment, anger, or hurt when you express what you are no longer willing to accept. The best thing you can do is prepare in advance how you will react if this happens—don't be at a loss for words!

The best thing you can do is explain your reasoning clearly and calmly, and emphasize that you're doing this because you care about your relationship. Express that you care about them deeply and you want the relationship to flourish, hence why you are setting some boundaries.

Confrontation Stage

Pick the Right Moment

Now that you've prepared yourself mentally, it's time to sit down and have that conversation! The key here is to pick the right moment when both of you are in a happy and calm mood. If this conversation is a result of their actions (in most cases this is accurate), then try not to schedule the conversation too close to the previous incident. You don't want them to feel attacked, and you certainly don't want to bring up the issue of boundaries in the middle of a fight!

Choose a moment when they're in a good mood and calmly ask them if they have a few moments for a quick chat. Don't make a big deal of it or behave as if they've done something terribly wrong.

Explain Clearly and Calmly

Next, state your boundaries as calmly and clearly as possible to them. Start by explaining why you want to introduce these boundaries and how they will positively impact your relationship. Starting on a positive note and in a calm manner will set the scene for a less confrontational discussion, not a perceived attack. While it's important to remain calm, you also want to get to the point you are trying to get across, so don't mince your words for too long.

You could start by saying, "I really want to have a quick chat to you about something that's been on my mind. I know that in the past we've had some disagreements and that's perfectly normal. However, what upsets me is when you raise your voice and swear at me. It makes me stressed out and I cannot communicate with you when you're shouting. I completely understand your emotions and they are valid, but I feel that we could really strengthen our relationship by expressing ourselves in a calm and respectful way. I really need this from you because I care about you and our relationship, and I don't want this to become a barrier."

By approaching the situation in this manner, you're expressing how you feel without attacking them or making it their fault. You're simply stating the problem, proposing a solution, and informing them of how you'd prefer things to be handled going forward. This is a much more effective means of conflict resolution, as you're also expressing that you care about them, but you also need your boundaries respected.

Stick to Your Guns

Now that you've said your bit, the ball is in their court as to how they want to take this new piece of information. If you're lucky, they may take it really well and agree to your new terms. If not, then they may try to make you feel guilty by manipulating your emotions into feeling bad about what you've said. This is where you need to be strong! Stand by what you said and don't allow them to sway your new boundaries.

Failing to stick to your boundaries will undo all of your preparation as your loved ones will lose respect for your initial efforts. Although this can be frustrating, you need to make sure that you remain strong.

The Aftermath

Persevere

Now that your boundaries have been clearly set, you can only sit back and observe. If your loved one continues to overstep your boundaries, then you'll need to stick to your follow-up plan that you thought of earlier in this chapter. The key here really is consistency—if you don't allow a certain behavior once, then you cannot allow it to happen again if you're too tired to stand up to them. If you show them that you are serious about these boundaries, then they will, over time, grow to respect them.

On that note, if you've told them that the consequences for a certain behavior will result in you stepping away from the situation temporarily or taking something away (if you're a parent), then stick to it. Do not give an angry ultimatum in the heat of the moment that you would never actually go through with, as you'll only lose their respect. When it comes to ultimatums, you need to think them through thoroughly beforehand and only say them if you really mean it, or else they're meaningless.

Do What Is Best for You

This next point is tricky, as it really does depend on the relationship you have with the person with BPD. Naturally, you cannot make the decision to cut out your own child from your life if they don't respect your boundaries (if they're under the age of 18). If the person is a friend or a relative, you do have the choice to remove them from your life if they continue to break your boundaries despite you having asked multiple times. In cases like this, it may be in your best interests to end your relationship with this person, or at least suggest taking a break.

Remember, nobody is holding a knife to your throat! You have the right to walk away from a situation that is harming your sanity.

Side note: If this is your child or someone you feel you cannot remove from your life, that's perfectly understandable. In a situation like this, your best bet is going to see a psychologist who specializes in BPD. They will be able to guide you through this difficult ordeal and propose alternative suggestions.

Final Note

While boundary setting is incredibly important, don't forget that you are dealing with someone with a mental disorder. Despite their best efforts, sometimes they lash out and lose their cool. You need to try and differentiate between them making a mistake, and deliberately continuing a bad behavior that you have confronted them about. This will depend entirely on the person and how well you know them, so you will have to use your own judgement. Lastly, always remember to reassure them that you care!

Chapter 7: Self-Help Exercises

Managing BPD can be a long and trying journey, but with the right mindset and treatment, it can be effectively managed. One of the many unsettling symptoms of BPD is dissociation, where the individual shuts down to the outside world as a result of a traumatic memory or being unable to cope in the present. Others may see it as daydreaming or being rude, but this is simply a coping mechanism used to escape uncomfortable thoughts or feelings. Dissociation can be voluntary or involuntary, and some are able to control it better than others.

If you struggle with this symptom as a result of anxiety or past trauma, then it may be a good idea to familiarize yourself with some grounding exercises to help you cope more effectively. Grounding exercises take a variety of forms and fall under a form of dialectical behavior therapy. These behaviors are categorized into different senses that you can draw on to self-soothe and distract, which will be outlined in this chapter.

Learning to Ground Yourself with the Five Key Senses

Sometimes all you need is some mindful acknowledgment of the world around you using the senses that your body naturally provides! The following are some of the best ways you can calm your BPD-induced anxiety naturally and effectively:

Auditory

One of the best ways to self-soothe and ground yourself when you feel as if everything is too much, is music! Prepare a playlist of all your favorite songs that make you feel happy and have it on hand. Load it onto your phone and keep it in your handbag with some headphones. Listening to good music when you're on public transport or going about your daily activities can really help to quell your anxiety and keep you grounded. You can also listen to DBT podcasts that are designed specifically for BPD symptoms and anxiety, and they are available widely and free of charge!

Calling a close friend or family member is also an excellent way to calm your anxiety and ground yourself. Even a short call of only a few minutes can make all the difference if you feel like your mind is shifting into a bad place. It's always a good idea to have someone you trust who knows what you're going through and is able to be there for you when you need it!

Lastly, if you have the opportunity, the best thing you can do is separate yourself from outside noise and sit in a quiet room for a bit to clear your mind. Sometimes you just need a bit of alone time to calm the nerves!

Touch

If you feel on the brink of a dissociative episode, grab a heavy, warm blanket and lie beneath it for a while, as this can help you to feel safe and protected while you settle down. If you have a beloved pet, having them sit by you can provide you with additional comfort and a sense of control. Whatever sensation helps you to feel the calmest should be your go-to, whether it's squeezing a stress ball, cuddling your pet, or holding a hot water bottle close (heat also has *amazing* calming effects). When in doubt, a hot bath or shower is a sure-fire way to relax and calm the nerves!

Visual

Find something around you that is aesthetically pleasing that you can look at to calm you down. It may be a painting of the sea or forest in your bedroom, or old family photos that bring back pleasant memories. These can all help to bring you an immediate sense of calm and comfort without much effort! You can also consider creating a Pinterest page with all of your favorite images or follow Instagram accounts with a collection of calming photos.

If you can, taking a trip to the beach or a large body of water is a sure-fire way to find immediate calm. Not only is the sea aesthetically pleasing, but the sound of the waves will also bring you a sense of serenity.

Taste

Taste is another powerful grounding tool that you can utilize to ward off a dissociative episode. Warm beverages such as herbal teas are excellent de-stressors, with chamomile being one of the most popular and effective for its natural calming properties. Bitter or sour foods are also said to help with anxiety! If all else fails, many people find chewing gum a really helpful way to eliminate any tension and keep you occupied.

One other food that is said to calm the nerves is chocolate. That said, don't overdo it with dairy! For the calming effects you'll need to stick to the darker variety, as it helps boost the happy chemicals in your brain which reduces anxiety levels.

Smell

One of the best things that you can do in and around your home is light an incense stick with a calming scent such as lavender. Alternatively, you can set up a diffuser and purchase a variety of soothing oils to enjoy the calming aroma. If the scents around your home aren't enough, go for a walk in nature and practice mindfulness. Take note of how the grass, trees, and flowers smell, and simply enjoy the present moment! The body is naturally soothed by nature. You'll be amazed at how effective it is!

Breathing Techniques to Treat Anxiety

One of the worst, yet most common side effects of BPD is severe anxiety and panic attacks. When this happens it can feel extremely scary and overwhelming, especially where you're unsure what to do next or who to call. It's not uncommon to feel frozen and unable to do anything, so your best line of defense is, in fact, yourself! Breathlessness is one of the main indicators of an impending panic attack, so learning to control your breathing is an excellent way to ward them off. That said, below I will be listing a few core breathing techniques that you can draw on to relieve stress and take control of your anxiety.

Learn to Breathe Properly

This is one common mistake that many people make when they practice deep breathing in an attempt to calm down! Many people breathe in as deeply as they can when they are feeling anxious, but this isn't doing your anxiety any favors. Why? Well, when you breathe in deeply you are activating your sympathetic nervous system, which is essentially your fight-or-flight response. This puts your body into panic mode and can actually *cause* hyperventilation rather than prevent it! The irony certainly isn't lost on me.

So, what does this mean? Well, you basically need to do the opposite if you want to calm yourself down and activate your parasympathetic nervous system. Instead of focusing on multiple deep inhales, focus on exhaling all the air from your lungs as slowly as possible and then inhaling. As a general rule, your exhales should always be a couple of seconds longer than your inhales. Next time you're feeling really anxious, try changing your breathing as described and notice how much calmer you feel! Approximately three to five minutes of this should be enough to bring you back to peace and normality.

Lion's Breath

Building more on the point above, this technique is donned the lion's breath and involves exhaling deeply and with force—as a lion would do!

All you need to do is the following:

- Sit with your legs crossed (the simplest way) or, ideally, you should be on your knees with your ankles crossed behind you and seated with your bottom on your feet.

- Stretch out your hands and arms, and slowly move your hands onto your knees and breathe in deeply through your nostrils, then exhale through your mouth with meaning and force.

- As you exhale, relax your facial muscles and place your focus either towards the mid-nose or forehead as you breathe out.

- Inhale once again and repeat until you feel completely relaxed.

Focus, Focus, Focus

For this next one, you'll need to find a peaceful spot where you can focus on tranquility and quiet. Before you start, pay extra attention to how you feel while you breathe normally. Take note if there is any tension in your body.

Here's what to do:

- Inhale deeply through your nose.

- Exhale deeply, releasing all tension in your body as you do so.

- Repeat this for a few minutes. Pay attention to the rise and fall of your upper body as you do so.

- Choose a phrase or word that brings you comfort and focus solely on it. For example, "peace and tranquility".

- As you breathe in, imagine the air you are inhaling into your lungs is a gentle ocean wave washing over you.

- Imagine your exhale as all your problems and anxiety leaving your system.

Building up to doing this technique for 20 minutes per day will make a huge difference in your anxiety levels.

It's All About the Abs

The most important aspect of relaxation breathing is the ability to inhale through your diaphragm; this helps you to breathe more deeply and requires far less effort.

Here's how you can practice breathing from your diaphragm:

- Start by lying somewhere comfortable such as your bed or couch.

- Place a pillow beneath your head and knees for extra comfort.

- Next, place one hand below your ribcage and another one below your heart.

- Breathe in and out through your nose, paying close attention to the rise and fall of your stomach and chest.

- Try and see if you can separate your breathing so that you are inhaling deeply into your chest.

- Next, see if you can do the opposite so that your stomach moves more than your chest.

- The aim here is to see if you can have your stomach moving more than your chest. It takes some practice, but it can be done!

Conclusion

Borderline Personality Disorder is one of the most misunderstood disorders, which is why it is so important to educate yourself. Whether you have the condition or a loved one does, it's important to understand how it works and the best possible treatment options so that you or your loved one can get the care you need and deserve. BPD does not have to be a life sentence if you receive the correct treatment and take the right medications. If you or your loved one have not yet received a diagnosis but you suspect that you may have BPD, it is strongly recommended that you go and see a professional. Regardless of the outcome, you will receive peace of mind in getting a proper diagnosis.

Lastly, and most importantly, understand that BPD is not a reflection of your soul and your intentions. It is an illness that deserves treatment just like any other. It does not make you any less of a person. Always be honest and truthful with those around you--especially yourself. Remember that you will have good and bad days. Appreciate the good ones and take the bad in your stride, and always communicate to your loved ones on the worst days. You're never alone in your journey, and you're stronger than you think!

References

Borderline personality disorder | NAMI: National Alliance on Mental Illness. Nami.org. (2021). https://www.nami.org/About-Mental-Illness/Mental-Health-Conditions/Borderline-Personality-Disorder.

Choi-kain, L. W., & Unruh, B. T. (2016). *Mentalization-Based Treatment: A Common-Sense Approach to Borderline Personality Disorder*. Psychiatric Times. https://www.psychiatrictimes.com/view/mentalization-based-treatment-common-sense-approach-borderline-personality-disorder.

Churchill, A. (2021). *9 Strategies for Supporting Someone with BPD | Crisis and Trauma Resource Institute*. Crisis and Trauma Resource Institute. https://ca.ctrinstitute.com/blog/9-strategies-supporting-bpd/.

David, N. (2020). *How to Set Boundaries with People with Borderline Personality Disorder*. Wikihow.com. https://www.wikihow.com/Set-Boundaries-with-People-with-Borderline-Personality-Disorder.

Legg, T. (2017). *Borderline Personality Disorder: Causes, Diagnosis, and Treatment*. Healthline.

https://www.healthline.com/health/borderline-personality-disorder.

Pugle, M. (2021). *Types of Borderline Personality Disorder Medications*. Verywell Health. https://www.verywellhealth.com/bpd-borderline-personality-disorder-medications-5100909.

Robinson, L., Smith, M., & Segal, J. (2020). *Helping Someone with Borderline Personality Disorder - HelpGuide.org*. HelpGuide.org. https://www.helpguide.org/articles/mental-disorders/helping-someone-with-borderline-personality-disorder.htm.

Salters-Pedneault, K. (2019). *9 Symptoms May Indicate Borderline Personality Disorder Diagnosis*. Verywell Mind. https://www.verywellmind.com/borderline-personality-disorder-diagnosis-425174.

Salters-Pedneault, K. (2020). *Schema-Focused Therapy Can Help People With BPD and Childhood Trauma*. Verywell Mind. https://www.verywellmind.com/schema-focused-therapy-425463.

Salters-Pedneault, K. (2020). *The Benefits and Risks of Mood Stabilizers for BPD*. Verywell Mind. https://www.verywellmind.com/mood-stabilizers-for-bpd-are-they-effective-425460.

Salters-Pedneault, K. (2020). *The Options You Have for Treating Borderline Personality Disorder*. Verywell Mind. https://www.verywellmind.com/borderline-personality-disorder-treatment-425451.

Salters-Pedneault, K. (2021). *What Are Common Triggers With BPD?*. Verywell Mind. https://www.verywellmind.com/bpd-triggers-425475.

Schimelpfening, N. (2021). *What Is Dialectical Behavior Therapy (DBT)?*. Verywell Mind. https://www.verywellmind.com/dialectical-behavior-therapy-1067402.

Smith, A. (2020). *Grounding Exercises for Individuals with BPD (Who Sometimes Dissociate) — Amanda L. Smith, LCSW*. Amanda L. Smith, LCSW. https://www.hopeforbpd.com/borderline-personality-disorder-treatment/grounding-bpd.

Smith, M., & Segal, J. (2020). *Borderline Personality Disorder (BPD) - HelpGuide.org*. HelpGuide.org. https://www.helpguide.org/articles/mental-disorders/borderline-personality-disorder.htm#.

Transference–Focused Therapy. Goodtherapy.org. (2021). https://www.goodtherapy.org/learn-about-therapy/types/transference-focused-therapy.

Wandler, K. (2020). *How to Overcome Borderline Personality Disorder | The Recovery Village Drug and Alcohol Rehab*. The Recovery Village Drug and Alcohol Rehab. https://www.therecoveryvillage.com/mental-health/borderline-personality-disorder/related/how-to-overcome-bpd/.

Printed in Great Britain
by Amazon